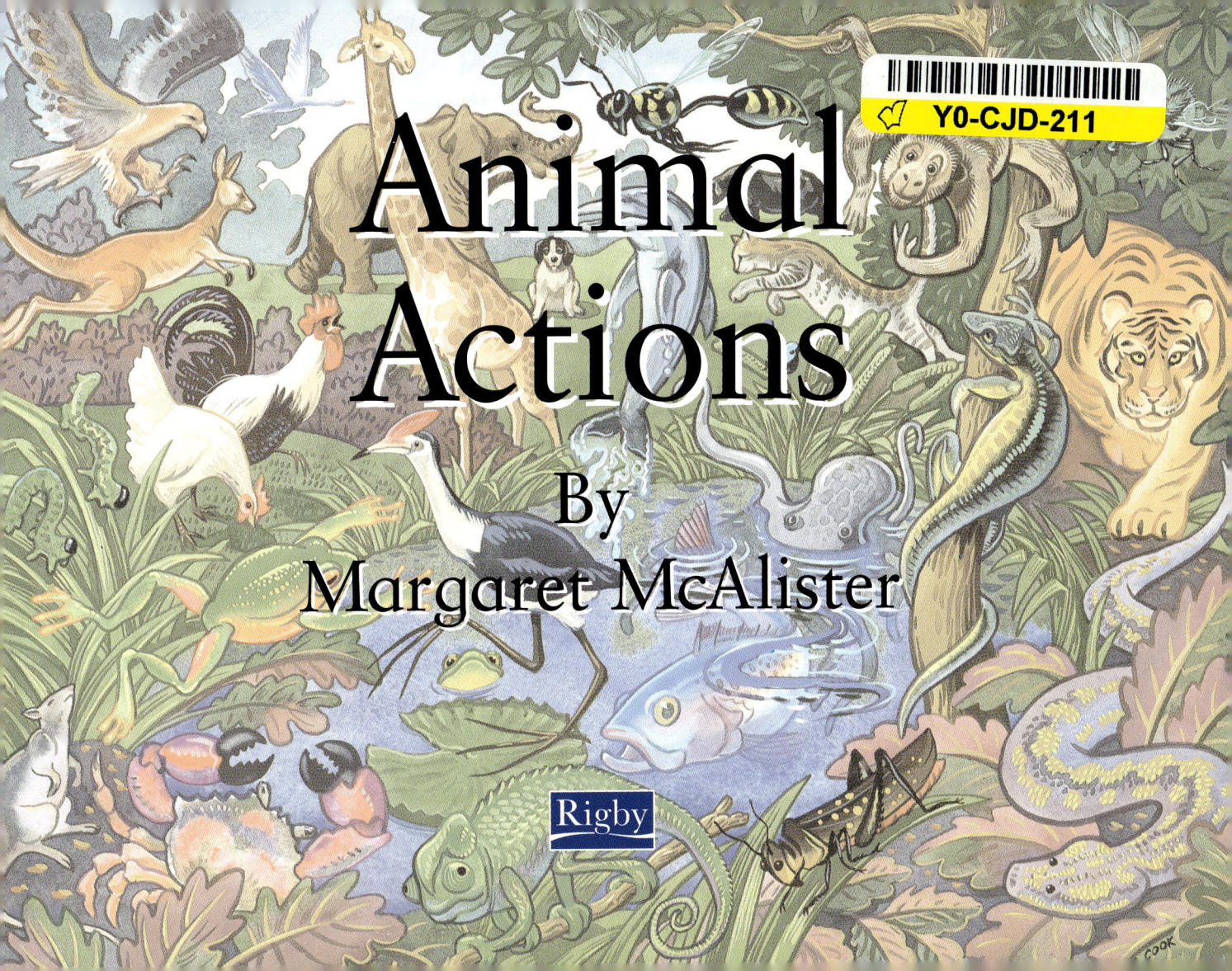

Not all animals move in the same way.

Some animals move fast, others move slowly.

Some swim, others fly.

Some crawl, others walk or run.

But all animals use two kinds of action to move forward.

They push backward with parts of their bodies. They also change their shape.

A lion walks by pushing its legs backward against the ground. Its legs and its body change shape.

How does this animal move?

This sidewinder snake slides forward by pushing its belly against the earth. It also changes shape.

6

How does this animal move?

A kangaroo jumps by pushing its legs backward against the ground. Its legs and its body change shape.

How does this animal move?

A snail uses its soft foot to grip the ground and pull itself along. It also changes shape.

How does this animal move?

This water boatman beetle pushes its back legs against the water like paddles. Its legs also change shape.

How does this animal move?

This bald eagle flies by pushing its wings backward and downward against the air. Its wings also change shape.

Elephants

Spider

Snail

Cheetahs

All animals use two kinds of action to move.

Index

beetle 11–12

cheetahs 15

eagle 13–14
elephants 15

kangaroo 7–8

lion 4

snail 9–10, 15
snake 5–6
spider 15